# DEVOTIONS for BOYS and GIRLS

# devotions

# for

# BOYS and GIRLS

By

## William L. Woodall

**Illustrations by Politzer**

ASSOCIATION PRESS     NEW YORK

Sixth Printing, October, 1961

 214

# Preface

I HOPE THAT this little book may bring you into a closer
relationship with God. For it is only as we know him that
we truly fit ourselves to live and grow here on his earth. These
are devotions to guide you in worshiping God.

Worship used to be spelled "worthship." It means to place
a high value upon some person or being. When we worship
God we are, in a way, stating just what God is worth to us.
We know, of course, that God does not change in value, or
strength, or truth, or love, or in anything else. But what *we*
think of God can and does change *us*.

These daily devotions do not follow any pattern. You may
use them at random or take them as they come. But as you
study the pages—the Scripture passage, the meditation, and
the prayer—always keep one thought uppermost in your mind:
God thinks you are important and he has great things in store
for you. He has put you here for a purpose and he has great
plans for your life. Get to know him and he will reveal those
plans to you. Use this book as a key to open the door to his
treasure house. "Prove me now, herewith, saith the Lord of
hosts, if I will not open you the windows of heaven, and pour
you out a blessing, that there shall not be room enough to
receive it."—Malachi 3:10

Yours for a glorious adventure,
WILLIAM L. WOODALL

# Contents

# 1
# A GLORIOUS ADVENTURE

## Read Matthew 13:44-46

There is a legend about some travelers who camped one night with a tribe of friendly Indians. Early the next morning—before daylight—the old chief came out of his tent to bid them farewell. He told them where to cross the river that bordered the camp and instructed them to fill whatever empty pouches they had with the magic sand of the river bottom. This sand, he told them, had strange qualities. It would make them both happy and sad.

Later in the day, one of the travelers quietly reached into his pocket and pulled out a handful of the sand. Wondering what the old chief had meant about being both happy and sad, he decided to examine the stuff more closely. To his utter amazement he found the sand to be flecked with nuggets of gold. Then the truth of the chief's words struck home to all of them. They were happy that they had found some gold, but sad that they hadn't taken more of the sand when they had the opportunity.

You will be like those travelers crossing that river as you spend time at school, in your club meetings, at camp, at church. Living is a glorious adventure. Each day brings some new treasure. Sometimes we recognize it, but too often we miss it. The secret of happiness is to look for something new each day and to make the most of each new friendship and each part of every day.

*Dear God and Father of us all, give us the wisdom to see our way through the happy days to come and the strength to make the most of every minute. We ask it in the name of Jesus Christ.* AMEN.

9

# RUNS, HITS, AND ERRORS

### Read II Timothy 4:7, 8

In a midwestern Christian university these words appear over the door of the gymnasium that leads out to the playing field: *Sixty minutes of action, no alibis, no regrets.*

It is more than habit that makes each player look up and read the words that he already knows by heart. Those words soon become a part of every player.

Sixty minutes in which each person will do his best to win for his school. Sixty minutes of real honest-to-goodness effort. Sixty minutes in which there is no opportunity to make excuses. Out there the player does what he thinks he has to do to win. If he makes a mistake, the whole team will feel it, and all the excuses and regrets in the world will not bring back one split second of that lost opportunity. That chance is gone, but he will have other chances—dozens of them—to profit by his past mistakes. He will be expected to do better next time.

Three things do not go in sports or in the game of life. One is cheating. Another is making excuses. The third is feeling so sorry that you can't think of anything else. Play the game for all you're worth and according to the rules. The final score will tell who is the winner, but how you act on the field will determine who is the victor.

*Help me, O God, to play the game according to the rules. Help me to win if I deserve to win. But, win or lose, please give me the satisfaction of feeling that I did the best I could at the time.* AMEN.

# NOTHING IS EVER LOST

**Read Acts 9:13-16**

Too often we think our mistakes cannot be made right again. Nothing is farther from the truth. God always gives us another chance.

While still a young man, the sculptor Michaelangelo used to walk daily past a discarded slab of marble that lay in a vacant lot. Two costly errors had been committed on that block of stone. First, the stonecutter who quarried it had cut it out too thin. Second, a great sculptor whom hardly anyone remembers today, failed in trying to carve a figure out of the piece. So it lay for one hundred years, waiting for someone to do something about it.

With considerable difficulty, Michaelangelo obtained permission to have the stone carried to his studio. For months he worked behind locked doors. The result made the Italian city of Florence gasp in wonder and amazement. From this supposedly useless, ruined piece of marble Michaelangelo had carved the statue of David the shepherd king of Israel—one of the world's greatest and most perfect works of art.

At the hands of a master a mistake was turned into perfection. How much more is God able to remake us than any earthly artist to work miracles!

> *O thou eternal Sculptor of the universe, help us to realize that it is never too late to turn again to thee. Make us truly sorry for our shortcomings and give us the strength that comes from faith in thee to start anew toward our goal of perfection. We ask it through him who never admits loss, our Savior.* AMEN.

# THE FRUITFUL LIFE

### Read Psalm 1

Change the first word of this beautiful psalm to "happy" and it takes on a clearer meaning for us. Not only is this a beautiful poem, but it offers some sound advice. It tells us how, step by step, to get the most out of life—now.

First, it warns us to be careful of our companions. If you really want to be happy, this ancient poet tells us, then don't even walk in the company of people who have no respect for God or what he stands for. For, he warns, if you walk with ungodly people you may soon find yourself standing with them. If you stand with them, it won't be long before you will be sitting in their councils, laughing at others who are trying to do what is right. But, he continues, the happy person is the one who likes to do what is right.

The psalmist lived in a dry, barren country, and the best earthly thing he could think of was a thriving fruit tree—thriving because it was growing beside a stream of fresh water. And that, he means, is what a person is like who shuns evil companions and their easy, glamorous ways. Do what is right and God will reward you for your efforts right here, today, and every day.

*O God, our heavenly Father, teach us the foolishness of evil ways. Sometimes they look so right, and those who practice them seem so happy. Guide us through the more difficult paths which lead us to the happiness of accomplishment and of knowing we are in the right.* AMEN.

**5**

# WHAT IS GOD LIKE?

**Read John 14:5-9**

Don't you sometimes wonder just what God is like? Then sometimes you wonder if it is right to ask questions about God. And then—let's be honest—don't you wonder in your heart if there really is a God at all? Don't be ashamed of your questions.

Oftentimes our parents and teachers and leaders can't answer our questions, and sometimes they will make us feel quite wicked for asking them. Jesus didn't get angry with his disciples when they asked searching questions. One of them, Philip, demanded point-blank: "Show us the Father [meaning God] and we will be satisfied." Philip and the others were puzzled about God and they wanted to see him right then and there.

Jesus told his followers that God is like himself. God, he told them, is loving and kind and understanding. You can't *prove* God. You can't argue about God. You have to feel him. When you thrill to a beautiful sunset or a stirring piece of music, that is God. When you feel, as you do some days, that everything is so very right, God is very near you. When you do something for someone without thought of reward or repayment, God is working through you. No, you can't point and say: "There is God." But God can point to you, and when he does you will know it.

*We thank thee, our heavenly Father, that thou art a God we can question as well as trust. Open our eyes and our hearts to thy presence, that we may know thee when thou art especially near to us. Help us to fill our doubting moments with beautiful thoughts and helpful deeds.* AMEN.

**6**

# YOU ARE WRITING A BOOK

### Read Matthew 5:13-16

If someone were to tell you that you are writing a book, you would probably think he was joking. Well, you *are* writing a book. It may not look like a library book or read like a school text, but someday someone is going to read your book. You see, YOU are the book that you are writing.

Each day of your life you are writing something in your book. Some days you may write only a sentence. Other days you may write a paragraph, a page, or even a whole chapter. Each day your book gets just a little bit longer and thicker as you do and say things that record themselves in the book of your life.

Your name is the title of that book. Your face is the cover; for whatever you put on the pages of your book will in some way appear on the cover. One time President Lincoln remarked to a friend that he didn't like a certain man because of his face. His friend was astonished at the great man's seeming prejudice and reminded Mr. Lincoln that the man was not responsible for his face. Mr. Lincoln replied that every man past forty years of age is responsible for his face.

Begin each day by planning what you will write in your book for that day. Make doubly sure that the pages you write will contain accounts of words and deeds of kindness, goodness, consideration for others, and thoughts of things that are high and noble.

*O Thou who hast also written a book, help us as we record each day's deeds. May they be great deeds and not things that will bring shame to us in later years as we leaf through the pages we are writing today.* AMEN.

# YOU ARE IMPORTANT

### Read Psalm 8

You are important because God thinks you are. The writer of the beautiful Eighth Psalm answered the question—"What is man?"—by stating that God made us to be just a little less than the angels and that he has crowned us with honor and glory. And more—he has given us everything in the world to use as we wish.

Now that is a pretty big place to fill, but that is how important God thinks we are. If God thinks we are "V.I.P.'s" (very important persons), who are we to dispute him? We do dispute his word, though, by being afraid to do what he expects us to do.

God expects great things of us, but he is not unreasonable in his demands upon us. He has given us minds and bodies with which to think and act, but he has given us more—the promise to be with us, to guide us and show us how we can fulfill his demands on us.

*Our God and heavenly Father, give us confidence in ourselves. Help us to realize that you are with us at all times to show us that we can do all things with thy help.* AMEN.

# IF YOU WANT TO BE GREAT

**Read Matthew 20:25-28**

Dr. Albert Schweitzer could have spent his life doing nothing but traveling all over the world giving organ recitals and making speeches. Instead, he prefers to live and work in Africa. Already an accomplished musician and college professor, he decided at the age of thirty to become a medical missionary. He chose Africa and set up a hospital in the jungle, taught the natives to read and write, and trained them as doctors and nurses to assist him in his ministry of healing.

One day, following a storm, he was repairing part of his hospital. He was hot and weary from lifting and carrying. He called to a native sitting under a tree to come and give him a hand. The husky Negro, whom Schweitzer had taught to read and write, rose to his full height and informed the doctor that he was a scholar and wasn't supposed to work. "Congratulations," laughed Albert Schweitzer, "once I hoped to be a scholar too, but I guess I didn't make it!"

Schweitzer, being great already, did not need to impress people with his greatness. But he became great by first being a servant.

*Gracious God, help me to ever be humble. May I never think myself too big or too learned to minister to my fellow men. I ask this through the Greatest of Servants.* AMEN.

**9**

# CHOOSING SIDES

**Read Joshua 24:14-16**

One of the most important things in life is the matter of making choices. In our games we "choose up" sides to make two or more teams. We choose what we are to wear, what we will do with our spare time.

Joshua, the leader of the Israelites and successor to Moses, put it up to his followers to choose whose God they would follow. The God of Moses and Joshua had brought them successfully out of slavery in Egypt and into the Promised Land. The journey had taken more than forty years and the people were weary of hardship and war. They were looking for "something easy." The religion of the people they had conquered was easy. God's way was hard.

How should we choose? Do we take a job because it offers more money or a better opportunity for service? Do we choose friends who always agree with us, or ones who have their own ideas and express them differently from us? Do we choose a subject in school or in scouting for credit or because we want to learn something? Sometimes we have to choose the hard way to get what we want.

> *Dear Lord and Father of us all, help us to make wise choices. Help us to make good choices. May we see the foolishness of choosing the easy way just because it looks easy. We ask this prayer through Him who chose the Cross.*
> AMEN.

# OUT OF STEP

**Read Romans 8:28**

A mother was looking at a picture of her son's infantry company marching for inspection. "Look," she beamed proudly to her friends, "they're all out of step except George!"

Another mother was asked how she maintained such an orderly home with such a large family of children. "Well," she said, "when one of them gets unruly or out of line I give him a dose of castor oil." Then she was asked: "But what if they all are bad at once?" "Oh," she quickly replied, "in that case I take the medicine myself."

When the whole world seems out of step with you, there's usually something wrong with you. When everyone disagrees with you, then you must be in the wrong. This doesn't mean that the crowd is always right, but when you think only you are right, it's time to re-think things.

The next time everyone else seems grouchy or touchy, be sure it's not yourself before you start to straighten them all out. When you find out who is wrong, then set about to change it— even if it turns out to be you!

*Dear God, give me sight to see the right*
*and strength to do it.* Amen.

# FRIGHTENING
# MICE

### Read Luke 2:42-52

You remember in *Mother Goose* about the cat who went to London to visit the queen. When asked what she did there, the cat replied, "I frightened a little mouse under her chair."

Here was a cat who had a very unusual experience—an opportunity to visit the Queen of England. There she did what she could have done in any farmhouse or barn in the empire. She frightened a little mouse. What a wasted opportunity!

When Jesus was twelve years old his parents took him to Jerusalem. Did he make a beeline for the carpenter shops, or look for things he was accustomed to see in Nazareth? Indeed not, he went to the Temple. There he stayed.

How do you spend your time on a trip? Do you read comic books while driving through strange country? Do you invent games to pass the time away? Or do you try to see all you can and learn all you can about the country you are passing through? Don't waste precious moments doing things you can do at home. Make the most of every new situation.

> *Our heavenly Father, we are grateful for the beauty and wonders of thy world. Teach us to enjoy every minute of every day of every adventure.* AMEN.

# FACE THE SUN

**Read Psalm 113:1-5**

About twenty-three hundred years ago in Macedonia there lived a beautiful horse. His name was Bucephalus (Beautiful Head). Not only could no one ride him, no one could even get near him. Then one day a young man decided he would master Bucephalus.

On studying the horse's habits the young man discovered that the horse was afraid of shadows. By patience and careful maneuvering, Alexander, who was later to be known as "The Great," kept both himself and the horse in such a position that their shadows fell behind them. They faced the sun, and the rest was a matter of good horsemanship.

Too often we are discouraged by shadows, and too often that is all they are. By keeping our faces to the sun, we become blinded to the things of life that are not important. We should not be ruled or frightened by shadows. The proper placing of light will put them in their proper places—behind us.

*Father of light, help us to live in thy light. May thy light so illumine our lives that all unimportant things will be seen for what they really are.* AMEN.

# RULES OF THE GAME

### Read Matthew 7:12

Every game must have its own set of rules. Each team and each player must abide by the rules of the game or the contest will end in confusion. It is just as important, also, that the game of life have its rules or the world will break out into utter confusion.

You will recognize our Scripture passage as containing the "Golden Rule" as given to us by Jesus. This is the rule of the game of life. People say it is impossible to follow this rule, or it is too difficult or too impractical. Therefore, we lay aside this rule and the result is crime, punishment, dishonesty, and, of course, war.

When the rule is broken, we don't really break the rule; we break ourselves against the rule. When we lay aside the rule, the game ends in a free-for-all.

Don't wait for the other fellow to begin using the rule. Start yourself. You may lose the contest but you'll win the game. You will forget the score by tomorrow. The victory will be a part of you.

*Our heavenly Father, help me to see the importance of the rule. Give me the wisdom to know that if I use the rule, others will, too. Grant me patience to wait for others to play by the Golden Rule.* AMEN.

# GOD IS NEAR

### Read Psalm 23

The Twenty-third Psalm is probably the best-known passage of Scripture in the entire Bible. But its poetic beauty partly obscures its great message—the nearness of God.

God is near. He is our shepherd, our keeper. He watches over us. He shows us where the green pastures are, where we can find abundance. He leads us beside the still waters. We can find refreshing thoughts where no danger lies. He anoints our heads with oil—a protection from natural ills and pestilences. He sets us down to a full table where our enemies can see how we are in favor with him.

Notice that God does not *remove* the dangers. The earth is not changed for our sakes, but by him we are guided to where abundance lies in safety. If God is with us, who or what can be against us?

*O God, our heavenly Father, we thank thee for thine everlasting presence. Teach us to know and recognize thy strengthening hand and make us grasp it.* AMEN.

# FOR THE HONOR OF THE GAME

**Read Mark 12:14-17**

Sports have had their share of brother acts. None is more thrilling than the friendly rivalry between the DiMaggio brothers, Joe and Dom. Back in Joe's big year he came up with a base hit for forty-four consecutive games, tying the record. One more game with a hit would establish a new record.

The fateful game was between the New York "Yankees" and the Boston "Red Sox." The DiMaggios were opposing each other in center field. Joe's first two tries were long flies which were easily handled. His third try felt like a homer and Joe felt victory in his grasp. It was a long fly to center field and brother Dom was nowhere near, but Dom *got* near it and made the catch of his career. Dom could have missed and no one would have been any wiser. Honor came first—the honor of the game—even before his brother's famous record.

The story has a happy ending, though. Joe connected with the ball on the fourth try for a homer and went on to fifty-six games for an unbroken record.

*Gracious God and Father, when I have to choose between the right thing and the popular thing, please give me wisdom and strength to do the right thing.*
AMEN.

# HOW TO DESTROY AN ENEMY

### Read Romans 12:18-21

If it weren't for our enemies in this world, life would be beautiful. Someone is always taking the joy out of life.

Our Scripture passage gives us a most effective formula for getting rid of our enemies. Most of us think we have a perfect formula for ridding ourselves of our enemies, but it is either illegal or un-Christian, or both. Anyhow, if we use our way to destroy our enemies, more of them will spring up.

Paul advises us to get along with those who oppose us. Don't wear yourself out thinking how to "pay someone back" for a wrong done to you. Paul assures us that God will avenge our wrongs for us and we'll feel a lot better in the long run.

The Christian way is to feed a hungry enemy, give drink to a thirsty one, be kind to all of them. We are not to make a show of friendliness, but do it naturally. Do the thing that the enemy needs most. Don't overwhelm him with kindness but strive to make his opposition to you look foolish in the light of Christian good will and fellowship.

*O God of love, remove from me the desire to strike back. Help me to bear my bruises and slights with a generosity that comes from following Christ.* AMEN.

# WHAT'S THE USE?

### Read Psalm 73

Does it really pay to try to do what is right? If you haven't heard or asked this question a good many times already, you will as you get older.

The other fellow's life looks so easy. We see so many people defying the law and getting away with it. People who never come near the church can be seen driving shiny, big cars and living in nice houses. We see boys and girls doing or saying evil things to gain popularity with the crowd, while others who try to do what is right are called "sissies," "flat tires," and "squares."

These things bothered our psalmist, too, until he went into his church and stood in God's presence. Then he saw things by God's light, and how different it all looked. These easy-livers stood in slippery places. Their happiness was all a mask. In fact, inwardly they were scared stiff!

God's good way is often thorny, rough, and steep, but it ends up satisfactorily. We achieve the victory by staying with God who "is the strength of my heart, and my portion forever."

> *O God, my strength and my redeemer, the way of the careless seems so right and easy. Show me early the true rewards of happiness that come from following thee.* AMEN.

# YOU ARE
# BEING WATCHED

### Read Ephesians 5:1, 2

Is there someone who is your ideal? Someone you'd like to be just like when you get to be his or her age? Do you find yourself imitating that person sometimes? Well, prepare yourself for a shock. Someone is watching and imitating YOU, too!

No, it is not just a silly idea. It is no more out of the question than what you are doing. Possibly your ideal has no knowledge of your feelings, either. That's why he disappoints you once in a while.

One day a little fellow was found by his mother crying as if his heart would break. Between sobs his mother discovered that he had heard the man at the service station across the street swear at a tire. The man had no idea he was being idolized.

As you live these days, wherever you may be, live, act, and talk as if you knew someone is patterning his life after you. For someone is. Do you want to be responsible for someone ruining a perfectly good life just because you became careless at a weak moment? Think it over. YOU are being watched!

> *O Christ, who should be the pattern for every life, stamp thy image on me. May the younger boy or girl who is watching me see someone worth watching.* AMEN.

# CAN DO

### Read Philippians 4:13

The U. S. Navy Seabees have a rather startling motto: "The difficult we do immediately; the impossible will take a little longer." Anyone who has seen this division of our armed forces at work will testify that the motto is not as flippant as it sounds.

These fellows whose favorite expression is "Can do!" showed the world an example of what training and confidence will accomplish. In the first place, their work lay in fields with which they were familiar—construction. They would construct a town to house a thousand people in a matter of hours. They removed or built hills as the case required. They would lay an airstrip in a jungle or a dock jutting out into a harbor. They were prepared to accomplish the difficult in a matter of hours. What appeared impossible to others sometimes required additional planning, but it got done somehow.

Now when Paul said that he could do all things through Christ who gave him the strength, the missionary did not mean that he was equipped to perform feats of magic. Neither Paul nor the Seabees could turn stones into bread or gold. But where God requires something of us, he will help us to do it.

*Dear Lord, our heavenly Father, much that I see to be done seems impossible. Sometimes I feel that time will not permit all that has been asked of me. Help me so to put my trust in thee that I will be able to do what is required of me. I ask it through Him who promised to help.* AMEN.

# THE GREATEST PRAISE

**Read Proverbs 27:2**

Everyone likes to be praised; it is a natural human trait. But praise comes in many forms and at unexpected as well as at expected times. Oftentimes we do something and forget about it, and how good we feel when someone discovers it and makes a big to-do about it. Sometimes we have to perform some task in the presence of other people and we enjoy their applause for a job well done.

One evening an entertainer was going through his paces before a group of servicemen overseas. It was an ordinary routine that the men had seen dozens of times before, and they took it very calmly. The entertainer, disappointed at the mild response to his efforts, stopped and began to clap his hands for himself. The audience "booed" him off the stage. That was rough treatment, but he asked for it when he tried to wring praise from the audience.

Just remember, if you do the things you ought to do, you are not doing any more than your duty. Don't expect praise for doing what any other person would do in a similar position. However, if you do something that is above and beyond the ordinary, your praise will come. Let someone else sing your praises; it sounds so much better that way.

*Dear Lord, our heavenly Father, grant me patience to wait for whatever rewards I may receive for the things I do for others. Help me to refrain from attracting attention to myself, and may whatever I do be done in a spirit of trying to make the world just a little bit better.* AMEN.

**21**

# THINK!

### Read I Corinthians 13:11

If there is any one power that God gave to mankind that sets him apart from and above the animals of the world, it is the power to *think*. Everything we see or do had its beginnings in a thought. The earth, the sun, moon, and stars, all began in the mind of God. He thought them out before he called them into being. The objects of man's hands are the results of thinking.

"I didn't think," says little Johnny, when he climbs up on the table and knocks over his mother's prize bowl of flowers. Which means that Johnny hasn't grown up yet. We all like to act and play like children sometimes. Even grown people like to let their mothers and fathers decide things for them sometimes when the going gets tough. But the more we let others decide the things for us that we should be deciding ourselves, the slower we will be in growing up.

To grow up, we have to *think*. Thinking is a part of growing up just as playing is, or developing our muscles. We develop our thinking apparatus by thinking, just as we develop our arms and legs by climbing trees, running, or mowing the grass.

Thoughtful people are happy people. When they make a gift to others, they think about what they themselves would like to have. The three-year-old will give his daddy a brightly colored ball for his birthday—something the three-year-old likes. The twelve-year-old will give something that they both can enjoy.

*O gracious God, our heavenly Father, help me to think. Help me to think how I sound when I speak. Help me to think how I look when I perform my tasks. Help me to think about others as well as myself. Help me to follow the Golden Rule.* AMEN.

# ONE THING AT A TIME

**Read Mark 9:33, 37**

Someone asked Will Rogers how he would spend his last hours if he knew he only had one more day to live. His reply was: "One at a time." How else, we ask, could he have spent his last hours, or any hours, except one at a time? But, even though we know we cannot spend them any other way, we don't always act like it.

Jesus and his disciples had a lot of work left on earth for them to do. In view of all this, he heard them one day arguing as to who should be the greatest in the next world. They were planning far into the future, and even beyond the grave, while there was much to be done here and now.

Will Rogers' answer wasn't so silly after all, was it? Each of us has about all he or she can accomplish in each day's tasks. And to do those tasks well takes patience and a certain amount of skill. We cannot do a good job here today if we are thinking about what we will be doing tomorrow. This doesn't mean that we should not plan for the future. Only the foolish do not want to think or plan ahead. But we are not supposed to be so anxious about tomorrow that we can't get things done today. Do you have an older brother or sister? Does their school work look impossible to you? Are they learning to speak French or Spanish and you can't make heads or tails of it? Don't let it worry you. It looked hard to them, too, once. But they took each day as it came and learned each day's lesson.

If we learn to live each day as it comes and make the most of every opportunity as it presents itself to us, we will never need to fear or worry about tomorrow.

*Dear God, help me to live each day as it comes. Make me thankful for each chance to learn or serve. Give me the mind and heart to do the tasks that are before me, and may I trust in thee for the future.* AMEN.

# ARE YOUR FEELINGS HURT?

### Read Romans 12:10

Have you ever watched a sunflower? Isn't it interesting how it faces the sun all day, following it as it crosses the sky? Then at night, when the sun goes down, the sunflower bows its head and waits for the sun to rise again.

Well, we are like that sunflower in that we are sensitive to things—both good and evil. We are sensitive to people who treat us kindly and we respond to them. But, at other times, we are sensitive to people who do not treat us kindly, whether intentionally or unintentionally, and we may be hurt.

Are you forever being slighted? If you are, perhaps there is something wrong with YOU. Did you ever think of that? Maybe you are getting your feelings hurt because you hurt other people's feelings. Not that they are "paying you back," but if you think ill of others, you will act in such a way that they will think ill of you, too.

In dealing with other people, try to think what you like to have done to yourself. Make sure that you're not hurting someone else's feelings. If you work hard enough at it, you may be sure that you won't have time to notice how many times your own feelings might have been hurt.

*Dear Lord, keep me so busy doing for others and saying nice things to and about others that I won't have time to imagine things that are not so. I ask this through Him who would not allow anyone to hurt him because he loved others too well.* AMEN.

# GIVE YOURSELF

**Read Matthew 25:31, 40**

In James Russell Lowell's great poem, "The Vision of Sir Launfal," Christ speaks these words to Sir Launfal:

> *Not what we give, but what we share,*
> *For the gift without the giver is bare;*
> *Who gives himself with his alms feeds three,*
> *Himself, his hungering neighbor, and me.*

The story goes that as the young Sir Launfal left his castle one beautiful summer day on his quest for the Holy Grail, the cup that Jesus and his disciples drank from at the Last Supper, he was greeted at the gate by a ragged leprous beggar. The knight tossed the beggar a gold coin without giving him a second look. Years later, on a cold Christmas night, Sir Launfal returned, cold, hungry, penniless, and was refused admittance to his own castle. There at the gate he shared the beggar's fire, and with him he shared his own crust of bread. They both drank from Sir Launfal's wooden bowl. When the bowl touched the man's lips it became the Holy Grail, and the beggar was revealed as Christ in disguise.

How often do we think of ourselves as doing great deeds in far-off places, when there is work to do right at home? To be sure, there is work to be done in foreign lands, but we must not be blind to the lesser tasks that prepare us for the greater ones.

*O loving and ever-present God, open my eyes to the opportunities for service that lie within call of my own doorstep. May I do the small tasks well before I reach out into the distant and unknown. Help me in little things that I may be prepared for the big things when they come.* AMEN.

**25**

# BE STILL AND KNOW

### Read Psalm 46

This Forty-sixth Psalm could very well be named the "noisy" Psalm, couldn't it? The psalmist brings in all the loud noises he can think of—man-made and natural. The world is a noisy place, when you stop to think of it.

But in the midst of all the tumult, the psalmist tells us to "be still, and know that I am God." In other words, let God talk to us in his way. Jesus told us to ask, seek, and knock. Sometimes, however, to hear God's voice we have to stop and listen, too. We have to pause sometimes in the midst of our busy, noisy lives and give God a chance to speak through the din. If we can find a quiet place, all the better.

After you have read the Forty-sixth Psalm, and have had your meditation and prayer, just lie still for a while and listen. Listen to the wind sighing in the trees. Listen to the lapping of the water in a nearby lake. Listen for the sound of night birds and insects. Listen to them all, and soon they will blend into a kind of song. Think of this song as the voice of God.

One of these times you'll hear distinct words, though maybe not often. But listen anyhow. Just know that God speaks in countless ways. He can't speak to you while you are talking or making a fuss. Be still, and know that God exists, and he'll make himself known to you.

*Dear God, our heavenly Father, I thank thee for the many gifts thou hast given me: eyes with which to see, a nose with which to smell, nerves with which to feel, and ears with which to hear the sounds of nature and of thy voice. Teach me how to tune my ears to thy voice and know when thou art speaking to me. Grant me patience to wait for thee. I ask in Jesus' name. AMEN.*

# JOHNNY'S HOME RUN

**Read Romans 1:16, 17**

As long as there are organized sports, the name of Babe Ruth will stand out as one of the greatest names of all times. It is likely that a hundred years from now there will be stories about his greatness—true or fictitious.

The Bambino, as his Italian admirers called him, will always be remembered because his heart was bigger than his home-run record. Once, upon arriving at a large midwestern city, the Babe was asked if he'd go to a certain hospital and visit a little boy who was dying of some strange disease. "Sure," said the Babe, "I'll go." It was good publicity too, but Babe Ruth didn't need any more publicity. He had plenty of that everywhere he went. He found Johnny Silvester pretty much as he expected—very sick. The Babe talked to Johnny, autographed a baseball for him, and did what he could to cheer him up. Then the big-hearted Babe asked Johnny if there was anything he could do for him. Johnny asked for a home run in that afternoon's game. Without hesitation Ruth promised it, knowing full well that no pitcher was going to "groove it" for him, either.

Johnny listened on his bedside radio to the game. Sure enough, the Babe connected with one and the ball went out of the park. A lot of things happened that afternoon because Babe Ruth was not afraid to promise to make good. The Babe got his home run which helped his record, kept his promise, and won the game for his team. But something else happened, too. Johnny Silvester got well. God used Babe Ruth to help cure Johnny because the great man was sure that he could do something if it was for a good reason.

> *Dear God and Father of us all, may I know that when I make a promise that is good and right, thou wilt see that I keep it.* AMEN.

# MAGIC WORDS

**Read Mark 8:5, 9**

In the *Arabian Nights* tales the magic words "Open sesame!" appear quite often to open up some secret cave or source of treasure. The Bible also has a magic formula, only there is nothing supernatural about our words. They open the mind of God. The words we use are "thank you."

When Jesus fed the multitudes on the hillside overlooking the Sea of Galilee he used only a handful of food. But the first thing he did was to give thanks. In our Scripture account we find Jesus with four thousand people before him and seven loaves of bread in his hands. There was no doubt in his mind that the seven loaves and the few small fishes someone else found would be enough. He knew beforehand that God would somehow see him through, and, sure enough, God did.

Notice that Jesus did not *ask* God what to do. He thanked God first, then set about to break the bread until all were satisfied. That is what we should do when we are confronted with some seemingly impossible task. If we have faith in God and give thanks to him, he will somehow see us through.

Try for a couple of days to be thankful for everything. Begin in the morning by thanking God for a bed to sleep in and for a good night's sleep. Thank him for the sunrise, breakfast, friends, for the sheer joy of living. Do that for a few days and see if God won't open something up for you. Don't tell God what you want him to do. Let him discover what it is you want and give it to you in his own way.

*Dear God, help me to say "thank you" more often. Help me to be more courteous and kind to those round about me, and may I be thankful and considerate to all who work to make my life more enjoyable. We ask it through One who was continually giving thanks.* AMEN.

# PEOPLE
# YOU DON'T LIKE

**Read I John 4:7-9**

Jesus once said that if we only like and do nice things for our friends and those who like and do nice things for us, we aren't doing very much to please God. The test of a true follower of his, Jesus tells us, is to be kind and friendly to those who we know can never repay us.

It is easy to be nice to people who are nice to us. Oftentimes we see people that we think we just naturally do not like. We try to avoid them. We don't like their looks, we say. But we have no right to judge a person because of the shape of his nose, the size of his mouth, the color of his hair or skin, or for any other reason that he cannot help.

How do we go about not disliking people? The first thing we can do is to try to understand why they act and look the way they do. Put yourself in their place and try to think how you'd act in similar circumstances. Then the most effective way to break down the barrier is to do something kind for that person. Why do all this when it is easier just to leave the person alone? It is Christ's way, and if we are followers of his we must imitate him. It will make you feel good inside, too. And that person might become your best friend.

*O divine Creator and Lover of all mankind, keep me from the error of looking on the surface of people. Show me how to see people as they really are. Make me tolerant of their faults as others must be of mine. Teach me to be kind to all of God's people. I ask this prayer through Him who loved me first.* AMEN.

# PROFITS AND LOSSES

**Read Luke 9:23-25**

Anyone who is familiar with the business world will understand the difference between profits and losses. A merchant buys things in larger quantities and gets them at a cheaper price than he has to sell them for. When he sells an article for more than he paid for it, we say he makes a profit. If he sells it for less than he paid for it, he takes a loss. A storekeeper cannot afford to lose more than he makes.

Sometimes, though, in our everyday living we are forced to take a loss in order to make a gain. If we rush in ahead of someone to grab the thing we are after, we may gain our objective but we will more often lose a friend. Sometimes we have to give something away to get something else. Christian living cannot always be measured by profit and loss in dollars and cents or in things gained or lost.

To be a follower of Christ, it is sometimes necessary to stand back and let someone else rush in ahead of us. We might see a chance to get something we have wanted real badly, but if we get it there is a possibility that we may hurt someone else. Getting what we think we want is not always the best thing for us.

Jesus warned us against dishonest dealings. He taught us that if we put first things first—if we put him first—we may find it hard sometimes, even costly. But in the end there is a satisfaction in knowing that we have done the right thing. Christ promised happiness to those who would forget themselves and follow his way. No other religion offers mankind so much happiness as Christ's way.

*Our Father which art in heaven, give me*
*the courage to follow Christ. Show me*
*what it means to deny myself and live*
*in and for him.* AMEN.

# GOD AND I

### Read John 5:17

Since God formed human beings and breathed into them the breath of life, man has worked side by side with God. Man is a co-partner with God in finishing the work of creation.

Once a clergyman was walking through the English countryside. He stopped to talk to a farmer who was working in the fields. Noticing how well kept the farm was, the minister remarked: "You and God have done a wonderful piece of work here." "Yes," replied the farmer, "but you should have seen this land when God had it by himself!" Maybe the farmer did have an exalted opinion of himself and what he had accomplished, but he did help God to make a farm out of some unused moorland.

When we plant a garden, we work with God. We are helping to beautify his world when we plant a tree or a bush or set out shrubbery around our homes. We help him when we keep the weeds under control. But we work for God in other ways, too. We work for him when we do a kind deed or lend a helping hand. When we speak a word of encouragement or praise to someone who is down on his luck, that is God working through us.

Yes, God can do a lot of things without our help, but we are useful to him in many ways. We are his hands, his feet, his eyes, and his voice in a lot of things. There are some things that God just doesn't do and we are required to do them for him. As you go through the day, try to think of the many things that you can do for God that he does not do for himself or for us.

*Dear God, it makes me feel important that I have been chosen to help you with your work in the world. Give me tasks to do and the strength to do them. I ask it through Him who worked with you to show us your love.* AMEN.

# GREATNESS COMES QUIETLY

### Read Luke 14:8-11

Do you daydream sometimes about how great you'd like to be? Maybe you like to imagine yourself a great ball player knocking the ball out of the park once or twice a day. Or maybe you imagine yourself an airline hostess calming people in an emergency or saving lives after a plane crash. Possibly you would like to be a great statesman or a great teacher, holding people spellbound while you talk. Well, it is only natural to have daydreams and you'll never be too old to have them.

Jesus understood this trait in human nature. He saw people rush in and grab seats at the head of the table at parties, only to be asked to give up their places to someone else. He saw how embarrassing it was to those who had to move down, and how important people felt who were invited to sit at the head.

Jesus tells us that he who would be great must first be servant of all, and that it is much better to earn your place than to try to get it by trickery or greed. People who set out to be great just for the sake of being great never make it. But if you want to be a leader in order to be of service to your fellow men, then greatness will come to you.

The great people of the world have first been servants. George Washington Carver was a slave and later a teacher before he became known as one of the world's great scientists. Florence Nightingale served as a nurse when it was not the accepted thing for a young society lady to do nursing. Livingstone chose to work among the Negroes of Africa, but greatness sought him out.

*Dear God and Father of us all, I would not be truthful if I said that I have no desire to aspire to some height. But help me to realize that to serve must come before everything else, and even though I may not be great, please help me to be useful.* AMEN.

# THE GREAT COMMANDMENT

### Read Mark 12:28-31

There is one big idea that stands out above all others in the New Testament—it is found in the word "love." It was because of God's love for his world that he sent Jesus into the world to teach us that God loves us. There is no other religion in which the idea of love is so strongly stressed as in our Christian religion.

The religion that Jesus taught was of the love of God for his creation. If, then, God loves us, we are required to love each other. It is our imitation of God that makes us his followers. Jesus taught us that we can imitate God, and he required of us that we should.

Can you think of any of the world's ills today that cannot be cured by love? Wars, crime waves, jealousy, greed—they are all brought on by lack of love. Even things like sickness, floods, and famines can be made less tragic by the application of Jesus' commandment to love one another.

Sometimes we wonder why people don't follow Jesus' teachings. His message is really simple. If people would love each other as they love themselves, how beautifully everything would work out for everyone. Think what that would mean. There would be no poor people nor slum districts. Wars would cease. Jails would be emptied. Everyone would have what he needed—if we would only obey Jesus' commandment to love one another.

*Dear Lord and Father of mankind, forgive us our foolish ways. Forbid us to try to make thy teachings appear difficult when thou has required that we become as little children. Teach us how to love each other even as thou hast loved us.* AMEN.

# CAN YOU
# STAND TO WIN?

## Read I Corinthians 10:12, 13

Do you know how to win? Winning does not necessarily mean getting the best score. But can you really and truly win without making your opponent feel like a penny?

All of us have seen contests that were hard fought and when the final point was made, the opponent would rush up and shake the hand of the winner. He is a good loser, we say. It takes a lot of strength to congratulate one who has beaten you, whether by a large score or a slender margin. But it is considered good sportsmanship to congratulate the winner.

But what about the winner? You have to know how to win in a sportsmanlike manner just as well as to acknowledge the other fellow as the victor. Do you gloat over your defeated opponent? Or even worse, do you try to be so "kind" to him in his loss that he'd rather you would not even mention it? Do you try to "advise" him on the game so he can be as good as you are next time? Or do you just grasp his hand and congratulate him on being a good player and a strong opponent?

Lots and lots of people can't stand success. If they suddenly become wealthy, they can think of nothing else. If they go to college, they think that no one else knows anything—even their teachers who also went to college! Believe it or not, success can be hard to take. When you feel success coming your way—whatever it may be—seek out God in a hurry and ask him to prepare you to receive it.

*O generous God, Giver of all gifts, help me to learn how to win. I think I know how to lose, but I need thy help in guiding me in my victories. May I be big in defeat and grand in triumph. I ask it through Him whose losses all turned out to be victories.* AMEN.

# USE IT WISELY

**Read James 3:2-6**

Did you ever stop to think what a wonderful gift God has given us in the gift of speech? We hear so many thousands of words spoken on radio and television every day that we begin to wish that there was no such thing as talk. But think how handicapped we would be without it. How wonderful to be able to express ourselves. How wonderful to be able to greet someone, to compliment someone, or to make our wishes known.

Our Scripture text gives us the idea that our tongues need to be bridled. Like horses, they need to be kept in control. An unbridled horse may be a beautiful sight to people who just naturally love horses. But an unbridled horse can do a lot of damage if he decides to go on a rampage. Tongues, like horses, need to be bridled. An unkind or harsh word can be apologized for, but it cannot be recalled.

The gift of speech is one of the important differences between humans and animals. But if we do not use our speech wisely, we are worse than animals who cannot talk at all. Speech is a God-given privilege and must not be abused.

As you go through a day, just stop and think each time you speak. Consider whether or not it is really worth saying or repeating. Do our words help or hinder, build up or tear down, kill or give life, hurt someone or give him a lift? Let us think a little more seriously about this precious gift.

*Dear God and Father of us all, I thank thee for the wonderful gift of speech. Help me to keep it wonderful by not using it too much. When I am tempted to repeat something that I think may be harmful to another, help me to realize that I am also hurting myself. Teach me to bridle my tongue and guide it, and not let it guide me.* AMEN.

# THE PERFECT CIRCLE

### Read Matthew 6:19-21

When the Italian painter Giotto was yet a young man his paintings were winning widespread fame for him all over Italy. He was kept very busy going from city to city painting his beautiful frescoes on the walls of churches. Today his paintings are over five hundred years old, and they can still be seen in many Italian churches.

One day when Giotto was painting in the city of Padua he had the usual gallery of onlookers watching him work. Suddenly there was considerable commotion outside and the crowd was forced to give way to an impressive delegation from Rome. It seems that the Pope had heard of Giotto's work and wanted some paintings done. He had not seen any of the painter's art, and the delegation had come to get a sample of Giotto's work.

Now Giotto painted on walls and he couldn't very easily send a church wall to Rome. So the envoys handed him a piece of parchment and directed him to draw his sample on that. He fastened the parchment to the wall. Dipping his brush into some red paint, he described a circle on the paper as perfectly as if he had used a compass. He handed the parchment to the Romans and went on with his work.

At first the envoys from the Pope were offended at the painter's insolence. But soon they began to realize that it was not insolence at all. Only a painter could exert such control over his fingers as to draw a perfect circle. They recognized the work of a master and they knew that the Pope at Rome would recognize it, too, when they told him how it had been done. Perfection in even little things is an indication of what to expect in greater works.

*Dear Lord, teach me to be careful in my work. Help me to realize that little things make for perfection but that perfection is not a little thing. May people learn to know me by my works, and may my works be worth knowing about.*
AMEN.

# PURE IN HEART

### Read Matthew 5:8

*My strength is as the strength of ten,*
*Because my heart is pure.*

These words which fit so perfectly into our Scripture verse were taken from Sir Gallahad's speech in Tennyson's *Idylls of the King.* The strength of gallant Sir Gallahad lay in the purity of his heart.

A group of boys were brought before a justice of the peace for attempting to break into a store. All of them were very frightened except one. When asked why he was not concerned about what might happen to him, he said that he was innocent and had nothing to fear. Later, when it was proved that he could not possibly have been at the scene of the crime when it happened, he said: "It makes you feel good inside to know that you're in the right."

It does make you feel good to know that you are right. Sometimes people are actually ill because of a guilty conscience. No medicine in the world will help them, and it is not an imaginary illness. It is just as real as a broken arm. People who are right with God and with the world are usually healthy people. Jesus said that if your heart is pure, you can see God. If you can see God, or see things in God's light, you will see everything right. You have nothing to fear. In the same poem Tennyson also said:

*Live pure, speak true, right wrong, follow the King—*
*Else, wherefore born?*

> *Dear God, I realize that only by the pure in heart may you be seen. I thank thee for the assurance that if I try to do what is right, things will happen right for me. But if it be thy will that I do have trouble, I'll know that I will be given strength to see me through.* AMEN.

# IT'S WHAT YOU MAKE IT

## Read I Corinthians 15:20-22

Alfred Nobel was a Swedish scientist. He experimented with explosives and invented dynamite. The invention of dynamite brought him a great fortune, which he desired to share with his fellow men. So he established prizes of several thousand dollars each for great discoveries in science, and for outstanding achievements in literature. Then when war came along and he saw how much destruction was brought about by his dynamite, he added another prize—for the person who made the greatest contribution for the peace of the world.

The Nobel Peace Prize is paid out of the profits realized from a power to destroy. Therefore, what was originally supposed to be for the good of man was turned against man, and once again turned for man. The law of gravity, which causes us to fall and hurt ourselves or brings airplanes full of people crashing to earth, is the same power that holds us on the earth and steadies our homes on their foundations.

The same raw materials which we can use to make something destructive can also make healing medicine. It all depends upon the way it is used. When the Mississippi overflows its banks, it brings destruction. When the Nile overflows, it brings life to the Egyptians.

> *Some ships sail east and some sail west*
> *By the self-same breezes that blow;*
> *It is the set of the sails and not the gales*
> *That determines the way they go.*

*O Creator of the universe, thou has made all things, and set all things in their places and moving things in motion. Teach me to use what thou has given me for the benefit of myself and my fellow men.* AMEN.

# TURN ON
# THE LIGHT

### Read John 8:12

If you have never been in an artist's studio, possibly you have seen pictures of them. They usually are on the top floor of some house or building with a skylight overhead. In order to see the proper colors and the proper shadows in whatever they are painting, artists want natural light—light from above. Artificial light makes false shadows and causes the true colors to appear differently.

Jesus said that he was the light of the world. He is the true light. If we see things in his light, we see things as they really are. Did you ever see a person carry a piece of cloth out of a store to look at it in natural light? They want to know how the thing really looks. So it is with the light that comes from Christ.

How do you use this light? Maybe you want something pretty badly but you haven't the nerve to ask God for it. Why? Because when you bring God into it, it just doesn't seem right somehow. You might be contemplating some deed that you are not entirely sure of yourself. Look at yourself doing that deed as if Christ were holding the light for you while you were doing it. Seen in that light, you'll soon determine for yourself whether it is right or wrong. Look at your friends—ask yourself if you'd be proud to introduce them to Christ. If you imagine Christ meeting them, you will know how they really look. Is a thing right or wrong for YOU to do? See yourself doing it with Jesus and get the real light on the matter.

*Dear God of Light, shed thy pure white light upon me that I might see the things around me in their true light. Help me to see the good things and the evil things as thy light shines on them.* AMEN.

# OUR FATHER

### Read Matthew 6:9; Luke 11:11-13

Did you ever think what you are actually saying when you begin to pray the Lord's Prayer? This great prayer, like so many things that we say and do over and over again every day, is in danger of becoming nothing more than a habit. This prayer is one of the grandest expressions of faith that man has been privileged to have.

Take for instance the first two words, "Our Father." God is *our* Father, not just mine, or yours, or his or hers. He is my father, your father, their father. That, then, makes us brothers and sisters, doesn't it? What, then, becomes of my dislike for people of other races, other nations, other religions? The men in jail, the strange peoples across the ocean, somehow bear a closer relationship to me whether I like it or not. The beggar at my back door, the pickpocket at the fair, and the urchin who steals milk from my front porch, all come a little closer to me.

The Lord's Prayer is not to be taken lightly. We should never say: "Let us *repeat* the Lord's Prayer." Christ did not give it to us to open and close meetings with. He did not teach it to his disciples to be used when their own words failed them. The Lord's Prayer is given to us by God as a right and a privilege to come to him and to ask him for our daily necessities. But, in order to get these necessities from him, we must remember that the color of our skin, the slant of our eyes, the texture of our hair, have nothing to do with his love for us. He made and loves us all.

*Our Father which art in heaven, I thank thee for the privilege of coming to thee in prayer. Keep me from vain repetitions. Make me to realize the full meaning of thy fatherhood. Teach me to live my prayers.* AMEN.

# DOES IT WORK?

**Read Matthew 7:15-20**

A little girl, taking her first Communion, was quite disturbed at the reaction she had to the experience. Before she had joined the church she watched her parents and other grown-ups eating the bits of bread and sipping the grape juice. Some cried, others just looked different, and some had absolutely no reaction at all. When this girl took Communion it seemed to make her bubble inside. And each time afterwards it was a joyous experience that stirred her up to want to go out and do great things.

Was the girl right or wrong? Our Scripture tells us how we can know whether these feelings are wrong or not. We are to tell by their fruits. If our religion bears good fruit, then it must come from a good source. If the source were evil, then the results would be evil. If the Lord's Supper just makes people more ingrown and sad, then those people are not getting the most out of it. If partaking of the Holy Sacrament stirs us up to want to get out and do things for the world, that surely must be considered "good fruit."

Jesus didn't come into the world to confuse the world or to give us a religion that children cannot understand. He came to make men and women, girls and boys, better people—and by being better, the world will get better.

*Dear heavenly Father, sometimes I get so mixed up when I think about religion. All around me I see people who are good on Sundays doing evil things the other six days of the week. Give me, I pray, a way of life that not only brings me happiness and a satisfied feeling, but will also make others around me happy. Help me to be fruitful.* AMEN.

# SIGHT AND VISION

**Read I Samuel 3:1;
Proverbs 29:18**

You watch a football or baseball game; you take a trip through the mountains; or you visit a large city. In these things you see many sights. Sight comes through the eyes. The reflection of light on objects causes us to see images as they are impressed upon the nerves of our eyes. That is sight.

Some people are deprived of their sight through some accident or deficiency. They don't see mountains or athletic contests or colors. But they do see visions. Eyes are necessary for sight, but something else is required for visions. Fortunate is the man or woman who has both sight and vision. Leonardo da Vinci, over four hundred years ago, had a vision of man flying by means of artificial wings. The Wright brothers brought that vision to the sight of the world.

If we lived only by our five senses we would not get very far. We must have visions as well as sight, or hearing, or feeling, or tasting. Without vision we will perish. We must dream or we will die. All we see is what has already been done. What we dream about or visualize is *to be* done. What we see and feel today was once a dream, either in the mind of God or of man. When we shut off our dreams we find ourselves shutting ourselves off from God. He is the source of our visions.

> *Dear God and Father of mankind, forbid it that I should put away my dreams —dreams of a world without disease or war, a world without hatred or jealousy. Give me visions of a better world, visions of actual things that the world needs, and visions of how I can help accomplish these things and bring my visions into reality.* AMEN.

# IT'S ALL YOURS

**Read Matthew 5:5**

When we think of a meek person we immediately think of Caspar Milquetoast. But meekness in the Bible has a different meaning. Can you imagine Mr. Milquetoast inheriting the earth? If he did, he would be so frightened he wouldn't know what to do with it. No, meekness is not being a frightened mouse or a human door mat. Such a person would not be worthy of inheriting the earth.

The old Jewish meaning of the word "meek" uses the idea of a mold by which God forms men. In other words, the meek are those who have been formed in God's way. They follow God's pattern. Meekness, then, could easily mean gentleness, kindness, friendliness, and a good many other creditable things. Blessed, then, are the God-people, for they shall inherit the earth. Blessed are the people who try to live after a pattern made for them by God. They are fit persons to inherit the earth because they are attuned to the thoughts of him who created the earth.

Jesus was meek, and so was Moses. No one walked over these two men; they knew God's ways. Knowing God's ways gave them a kind of gentleness and sweet temper that people often mistake for weakness. Meekness is not weakness. It is the strongest trait a person can have, because it means putting one's trust in God and in making oneself after God's pattern.

*Dear heavenly Father, thy promises are more than we can understand. Forgive us for living in darkness and poverty when we could, with thy help, inherit the earth. Make us grateful for thy gifts already bestowed, but prepare us for the gifts to come when we give ourselves to thee.* AMEN.

# TEACH US TO PRAY

## Read Luke 11:1-4

Prayer is the very lifeblood of faith. Without prayer our faith will wither and die, and if our faith is gone, there is nothing left for us to live for. Jesus' disciples realized this and asked their Master to teach them to pray. We, too, want to know how to pray.

Jesus tells us first to address God. By doing this, we realize to whom we are speaking. When we talk to God we must be absolutely honest. When we say, "Hallowed be thy name," we are acknowledging that prayer is serious business and we must pray honestly or not at all. When we realize fully that it is really God to whom we are talking, then we take prayer seriously.

Jesus taught his disciples to pray for necessities. He taught them to pray for forgiveness. But before God will forgive, we ourselves must forgive those against whom we are holding some grudge. Prayer is a two-lane highway to God and back again. We open our hearts to him on our lane; he instructs us on his lane. We don't instruct him. Prayer is getting in tune with God's voice. Once we begin to receive messages from him, we are really and truly praying.

*This time, make your own prayer. First, address God by naming him and calling him by one or more of his acts, such as Creator. Ask forgiveness for your sins and shortcomings—not just for the wrong things you have done recently, but also for the things you have not done that you should have done. Now, thank him for some of the things he has done for you. Ask him to make you worthy of those gifts and more to come. Ask him for something. Offer to help one of his creatures. Ask for guidance. Pray for another person. Ask it through Jesus.*

# AS OTHERS SEE US

**Read Matthew 7:1-5**

*Oh wad some power the giftie gie us*
*To see oursel's as others see us!*
*It wad frae monie a blunder free us,*
*And foolish notion.*

These well-known words of Bobby Burns spoken to a louse are soul-searching words. I wonder if he really wanted to be given some power in order that he might see himself as others see him. Do any of us have the courage to face that bit of knowledge?

First of all, then, we should not be too critical of other people. Jesus tells us not to judge others when we are in need of standing in judgment ourselves. Why, he asked, do you look so hard at the speck that is in thy brother's eye when you have the undergirdings of a house in your own eye? Those are pretty hard words.

We spend a lot of time before a mirror making faces or combing our hair, but do we ever talk to ourselves in the mirror? Oh yes, we tell ourselves we are pretty great stuff, but do we ever ask ourselves embarrassing questions? Do we dare ask ourselves what other people actually think of us? A person needs to know what others think of him once in a while in order to straighten himself out. Maybe we don't like what others think of us. If we don't, then it is our job to make ourselves so likable that we don't need to fear what others think.

*Dear Lord and Father of mankind, forbid it that I should ever again fear to hear the truth about myself. Help me so to live and talk that I do not need to fear what people are saying about me. In the meantime, O God, help me to withhold judgment of others. AMEN.*

# HAVE COURAGE

### Read Joshua 1:6-9

Do you remember the lion in *The Wizard of Oz?* What a sad spectacle he was—a lion without courage. He tried to frighten others, but when they turned on him he was frightened nearly out of his hide. In other words, he was a coward.

Joshua had a big job to do. He was to take Moses' place as leader of the children of Israel. God told him to have courage because he would be with Joshua. If anyone needed courage at any time, Joshua did when he took over a grumbling nation of people and prepared to lead them into a strange land with hostile people waiting for them.

But courage is found in other circumstances than in bullying people or in leading armies into battle. It takes courage to face up to a crowd that is bent on doing something wrong or foolish. It takes courage to say No when it would be easier and more popular to say Yes. It takes courage sometimes to say Yes when we know that what we are promising to do will mean sacrifice of time and strength. It takes courage to volunteer to help others. It is a lot easier to sit on the sidelines than to be in the planning and carrying out.

Courage is needed in this world today. People are madly trying to get something for nothing. But the world is not made that way. Someone has to stand up and be counted on the side of right. Some day you are going to be called on to have courage.

*Dear God and Father of us all, give me courage to do the right thing. Even if it means going against the crowd, O God, help me to do what is right. Give me courage to live.* AMEN.

# GOD'S REQUIREMENTS

## Read Micah 6:8

Do you get confused sometimes and wonder just what it is that God really wants us to do? Any thinking person does. In Micah's day, people tried to please God by burning sacrifices on religious altars. People today think they are pleasing God by going to church on Sunday—when they feel like it. Some people try to please God by making certain motions or by observing some ceremony. If these things make people better, well and good, but they are not the most important things that God wants us to do.

Micah said that God wants us to do justly. Don't take advantage of the weak or blind, or of people less intelligent than we are. He wants us to be fair in our dealings with other people.

God wants us to be kind to people and not to cheat them. Show mercy to those who need mercy. If someone owes you some money or a favor, don't press him too hard. Don't, said God, go to court with your differences, but be considerate and merciful and things will work themselves out.

God wants us to be humble and walk with him. But, we protest, it is an honor to walk with God. Maybe it is an honor, but it isn't always easy. To walk humbly with God means going the whole way with him and not turning off at the first green meadow we see. It means putting our wants and desires in second place. It means putting God first. That is the way we please God.

*Our Father in heaven, I thank thee for making me a follower of thine. Now help me to see my duty to thee and help me do it with strength and dignity. Help me to do justly, love mercy, and humbly walk with thee. We ask it through Him who found the way of life for us.*
AMEN

# MY BROTHER'S KEEPER

**Read Genesis 4:9, 13**

This Scripture reading tells about the first crime committed on the earth. A man killed his brother. When God came to earth to ask where Abel, the slain brother, was, Cain asked God if he was his brother's keeper. God didn't answer him because Cain knew what the answer was when he asked. It was: "Yes, you are your brother's keeper."

A little girl was carrying her brother across a creek on her back. A man passing by and watching them remarked, "That's a big load for a little girl." "Oh, but No," the girl answered, "he's not a load, he's my brother." We *are* our brothers' keepers. We were put on this earth to do the will of God, and not just to please ourselves or to destroy what we think we don't like.

God provides for us above and beyond what we need. Some of us have more than others. But some unknown cause which we cannot understand deprives millions of others of the bare necessities of life. Are we responsible for them? If we ask that question, we already know that we are responsible.

God has made this world in such a way that each and every one of us has a duty to perform. Some duties are more demanding and far-reaching than others. But we all have our jobs to do. We are responsible for the welfare and comfort of others. Let us never grow so hardened to the needs of others that we fail to see our duty.

*Our kind heavenly Father, I know I am my brother's keeper. But I find it hard sometimes to stop what I'm doing so that I may help others. Give me the vision of service and the feeling for the well-being of others that a true follower of thine must have.* AMEN.

# ECHOES

### Read Ecclesiastes 11:1-4

A little boy had just discovered that wonderful thing in nature called an echo. After calling all the greetings he could think of, he began to shout phrases. His good phrases ran out and he shouted things like "Get lost," "Go home," and "I hate you." When those words came back so clearly, he was disappointed with the echo.

But isn't an echo a real part of our lives? It throws back at us just what we have sent out. If we give out kindness, then kindness comes back. If we send out meanness, we get the same in return. We don't always like what we get back, but maybe others don't always like what we give, either.

Our text from Ecclesiastes tells us that we get out of life just what we put into it. By casting bread upon the waters, the writer meant sowing wheat where it would be watered well. For instance, when the Nile River overflows its banks, then is the time to sow. One might think that the seed would be lost. However, after many days it grows and produces manyfold. Also he tells us to do good to seven, the complete number, or everyone—or even to eight, better than everyone. Then when we need help, good will come back to us.

That is the way of this world. We have to do for others if we are to be done for, to praise if we are to be praised, to please others before others will try to please us.

*O Lord God, it is hard for me to do good and to forget about it. Help me to want to do things for others. I want others to do things for me, but make me do those things for them first — and do them for the joy there is in it for me just to serve others.* AMEN.

# IT MIGHT HAVE BEEN

**Read Luke 12:16-21**

*For of all sad words of tongue or pen,*
*The saddest are these: "It might have been!"*

Yes, those are sad words: "might have been." There is not a much sadder sight in the world than a person who has wasted his or her life. Someone said that the sad thing about youth is that it is wasted on young people. But the fact is that you have youth only while you are young. Isn't it a shame that more people do not realize what a grand experience it is? Instead, most young people wish they were older—sixteen, so they can drive the family car; then twenty-one, so they can get away from their parents' bossing. Only they find that after they are twenty-one they have more bosses than ever!

The happy person ten years from now will be the person who makes the most of life today. If you slip a comic book inside your geography to fool the teacher, you are only fooling yourself. Lots of people have done just that before you, and now they can't read a road map or give sensible directions when asked. If you fool around when you should be studying, you are cheating yourself out of much needed and useful knowledge.

Today is the time to start enjoying tomorrow; for tomorrow starts today. So live and prepare yourself that when that big chance comes, you'll be ready to grab it. Have fun? Sure, by all means, but remember to save some fun for tomorrow by earning or learning something today.

*Our Father which art in heaven, I see all about me people who are disappointed because they are not what they once hoped they would be. Please, I pray thee, keep me from that error. Teach me to make the most of every precious day.*
AMEN

# GETTING THE MOST FROM GOD

### Read Psalm 67

The writer of the Sixty-seventh Psalm did not mince words about what we can expect from God if we follow a certain pattern of belief and behavior. There is little that we can do for God except help his creatures. God is no doubt pleased with our ways when they are good and constructive, when we lend a helping hand to one of our fellow beings, but whatever we do does not in any way change him.

The psalmist tells us that we can expect great things from God if we will praise him. This doesn't mean that God is a vain old man who requires us to say nice things about him. But by praising him we are committing ourselves to his greatness, and by admitting that he is great we are making ourselves receptive to his countless blessings. By failing to praise or to acknowledge God we are shutting out his light and holding off his great source of supply that is ever in readiness for us.

What we believe about God largely determines what we ourselves are. A nation that denies his existence is a sorry nation. A nation that thinks he is only a God of war makes a miserable neighbor. The jungle savages that believe God is some changeable being whom they must be continually soothing by rituals and sacrifices live lives of abject terror. If you want to get to know God, then praise him. If you want his blessings as his earth yields her increase, then be thankful unto him and praise him. The stronger your love for him and your belief in him, the more abundantly will he bless you.

*Dear God and Father, help me to more fully understand your plan for me. Help me to be grateful for all you have done and will do for me. I know I cannot do anything that will change you, but I can do things that will please you. Show me what I must do to enjoy your blessings.* AMEN.

# GREAT DAY

### Read Psalm 118:5-9

There is a popular song that makes the rounds for a while, fades away, and then comes back again in all its glory. It runs something like this: "When you're down and out, lift up your head and shout: 'There's gonna be a great day.'" We all get a lift out of the stirring tune, but we shouldn't forget the words, either.

Yes, there's going to be a great day. It doesn't have to be "beyond the Great Divide," either, as the cowboy sings. It can be here and now—today or any day.

There are many cures for the blues, and the one the psalmist recommends here is to call upon the Lord in the time of your distress. He will answer you just as he answered the ancient poet of Bible days. The poet says, "He set me up in a large place." God will do just that for you if you give him a chance.

When things seem to be going against you, when it seems that you got up out of the wrong side of the bed in the morning, when you drop everything you pick up, when you run at cross purposes to your parents, teachers, monitors, and a dozen other people you have to try to please—when these things happen singly or all at once, just lift up your head and say to God and to yourself: "There's going to be a great day." Then start to live as if that day is starting right now.

*Dear God, our heavenly Father, I thank thee for the knowledge that I have a friend in heaven who knows and understands me. Keep me free and happy, but when I get the blues, please remind me that thy help is always available. I ask it through Him who constantly sought thee.* AMEN.

# PRACTICE POISE

**Read Acts 7:54-60**

Don't you admire a person with poise, someone who can stand up straight and look another in the eye and express his views without stammering or getting excited? We've all seen people like that. Mostly, though, we see them in the movies or on television.

We know, of course, that play actors can look one way on the screen or stage and act quite the opposite in real life. But some people do have a lot of poise. With some of them it comes naturally; with others it has been developed. Sometimes they use poise to cover up fear or a feeling of insecurity.

A much more satisfactory way to have poise comes through trust in God. That is what Stephen had. Through his trial and execution he never lost his temper or his bearing. With his dying breath he called out to God to overlook the incident of the stoning as far as the killers were concerned. That takes poise.

That kind of poise and bearing comes only from God. The Christian has it in the marrow of his bones and in the color of his blood. It is a part of him and it cannot be taken away. Try trusting in God the next time your patience is being tried or when you are being humiliated. If you are in the right, take satisfaction in knowing that you are right. Talk it over with God. You, too, will be cool and poised.

*Dear Father God, sometimes my patience is tried to the breaking point. I want to be able to live in this topsy-turvy world and not become a part of its confusion. Speak to my soul. Strengthen my being. Instill in me that love of thine which passes all understanding or knowledge. Help me to have the poise of Christ and his followers.*
AMEN.

# THE BEST
# IS YET TO BE

**Read Psalm 37:23-25**

> *Grow old along with me!*
> *The best is yet to be,*
> *The last of life, for which the first was made.*

These great lines from Robert Browning's *Rabbi Ben Ezra* give additional meaning to much that we read in the Bible about the progress of life. When we are young we don't think very much about getting old. But in later years some people dread getting old. They dye their hair and color their cheeks, trying to fool Time! The Bible tells us that we should not fear getting older. When we can no longer run and jump, we can take pleasure in watching others do the things we once did.

Our youth is the preparatory time of life. Our games develop our muscles just as a crying baby is developing his lungs. Then a day will come when we will enjoy looking back on these things as well as doing things that older people do. The more things we do and enjoy today, the more fun we will have when we progress to other things.

Do not be afraid of the future—how you will look, where you will live, where and how you will work, what kind of friends you will have. Make each day a glorious experience. Do all the things you can do. Make all the friends you can make. Learn all the things you can learn. Life is like a savings account. The more you store up in love, service, and knowledge, the more you will have to use later on.

*Dear Lord of life, I thank thee for these days. Help me so to live that each day will add to the day before. Trusting in thy love and mercy for me, may I never fear what the future will bring. May I realize that so long as you are there everything will be all right.* AMEN.

# HOW HIGH IS THE SKY?

### Read Psalm 19

If all the stars in the universe, excepting our sun, were to go out suddenly tonight and never shine again, it would be eight years and nine months before anyone on earth would know it. When we think that light travels at the rate of 186,000 miles per second (that's seven times around the earth in less than two heartbeats) and that the light of Sirius, the nearest star, takes eight years and nine months to reach us, we begin to think how magnificent God really is.

Yes, the heavens declare the glory of God. Look up at the sky tonight and find the Big Dipper. Then let your eye follow the three stars that make up the handle of the Big Dipper. When your eye comes to the last star, then follow that same line to the next bright star. That is Arcturus. The light from Arcturus that you see tonight started "coming down" forty years ago. Millions of others, of course, are much farther away than Arcturus.

God is so magnificent that it is impossible for man to imagine just how great he really is. We can make ourselves dizzy just thinking about the magnitude of the universe. It has no end! How could it? If it ended somewhere, what's on the other side? When did *time* start? If you can make a guess as to when it did, then try to think what there was before time. Man still has a lot to learn about the universe.

But with all God's magnificence and grandeur, we are his pride and joy. He gave us many, many things and is constantly unfolding many more things before our eyes. Some things we may never know. But, strangely enough, the more mystery we run into, the more respect we have for God.

*Dear God, I feel so small in the presence of thy creation. But I thank thee, that in all of it thou hast given me a place of importance.* AMEN.

# PILLAR
# OF FIRE

### Read Exodus 11:20-22

One of the most gigantic undertakings in the history of man was accomplished by Moses in moving the children of Israel out of Egypt and toward the Promised Land. The Bible tells us that there were 600,000 men as well as the women, the children, and the cattle.

But Moses knew that he was acting under orders from God. Historians say that such a pilgrimage was impossible from a number of different standpoints. They do not consider the fact that God was there. God *was* there and Moses knew it. Constantly before them was a pillar of cloud by day and a pillar of fire by night.

Think what these signs of God must have meant to these people, especially at night. The pillar of fire gave them light in the darkness—light to see by and light to live by.

God is with us today. He lights our way. He guides us. He gives us orders that would seem impossible to many; but to those who know and trust him, they are orders that can be followed. God never leaves us alone to fight a thing through by ourselves or to struggle against odds without his help. He is there in one form or another—as a pillar of cloud or fire, in a friendly breeze, in an extra burst of strength, in the spoken word of a parent or friend, or in a still, small voice of encouragement that only we can hear when we need it. Let us watch for some sign when we feel alone while working for God.

*Dear God, I thank thee for thine eternal presence. May I never feel alone while I know thou art near. Help me to feel thy presence as strongly as any other being. I ask it through Him who said he would always be with me.* AMEN.

# AS YOU WISH

### Read Matthew 7:24-27

Two boys were exploring the woods at the foot of a mountain and they captured a bird that was too young to fly. "Let's have some fun with the Old Man of the Mountain," one of the boys said. "We will take the bird to him," he continued. "I'll hold it in my hand and ask him what I have. He'll know the answer because he seems to know everything. Then," he said with a twinkle in his eye, "I'll catch him. I'll ask him if it is a live bird or a dead bird. If he says it's alive, I'll squeeze it to death. If he says it's dead, I'll let it fly away." "That will be fun," said the second boy. "Let's go."

They found the Old Man of the Mountain sitting by his cottage. "Old Man of the Mountain," said the first boy, "what do I have in my hand?" "You hold a little bird, my son," was the reply. "But, tell me, Old Man, is it alive, or is it dead?" The Old Man looked the boy in the eye for a moment. Then he said: "As you wish, my son. Just as you wish."

Your life will be just what you choose to make it. It is entirely *as you wish.*

*Our Father which art in heaven, help me to build my house of life on solid rock. Give me the strength necessary to withstand the storms of life. Help me to make it a glorious adventure. May I never get bored with living. I ask it through Him who promised that life should never get tiresome or boring.* AMEN.